ON PURPOSE

ON PURPOSE
Towards a More Meaningful Life

SELECTIONS BY MARGARET GEE

FOREWORD BY BRADLEY TREVOR GREIVE

NEW HOLLAND

First published in Australia in 2004 by
New Holland Publishers (Australia) Pty Ltd
Sydney · Auckland · London · Cape Town

14 Aquatic Drive Frenchs Forest NSW 2086 Australia
218 Lake Road Northcote Auckland New Zealand
86 Edgware Road London W2 2EA United Kingdom
80 McKenzie Street Cape Town 8001 South Africa

Copyright © 2004 in text: Margaret Gee
Copyright © 2004 New Holland Publishers (Australia) Pty Ltd

All rights reserved. No part of this publication may be reproduced, stored in a retrieval system or transmitted, in any form or by any means, electronic, mechanical, photocopying, recording or otherwise, without the prior written permission of the publishers and copyright holders.

National Library of Australia Cataloguing-in-Publication Data:

Gee, Margaret.
On purpose : towards a more meaningful life.
ISBN 1 74110 143 3.

1. Quotations. 2. Celebrities - Quotations. I. Title.

080

Publishing Manager: Robynne Millward
Project Editor: Glenda Downing
Internal Design: Joanne Buckley/Karlman Roper
Cover Design: Joanne Buckley
Production Manager: Linda Bottari
Front cover photograph: Getty Images
Printer: Tien Wah Press (Pte) Ltd, Singapore

10 9 8 7 6 5 4 3 2 1

The author will be making a significant donation to the Taronga Foundation and the Australian chapters of UNICEF and Amnesty International.

For the people of Bhutan—
Namé samé kadin chhé—
thank you beyond the sky and the earth.

FOREWORD

At times my friends and I have enjoyed playing simple intellectual games, such as choosing one person and one item to take to a desert island where you will spend all eternity. Most responses are froth and wit, and nothing more, but every now and then someone brushes against the very essence of the greatest problem we face: What is it that matters most to us? From what do we derive true meaning?

I was quite alarmed when Margaret Gee asked me to put to paper that which has brought me the most meaning in my life. I daresay my more celebrated co-contributors felt similarly ill at ease at such a daunting prospect. However, the process of sifting through my most precious experiences to determine which was the most fulfilling has been thoroughly invigorating.

I have greatly enjoyed reading the thoughts of many remarkable individuals I have long admired. Some are as reassuringly unsurprising as they are inspiring. General Peter Cosgrove champions a straightforward belief in integrity as a method of bringing and binding people together in a way which would be impossible alone. Chess supremo Garry Kasparov speaks of the importance of total immersion in everything he does, while flamboyant adventurer Sir Ranulph Fiennes offers a startling shellfish aphorism about humility and the getting of wisdom.

William Dalrymple, with typical British understatement, simply reminds us that, 'there are many roads up the mountain', and I knew exactly what Naomi Wolf meant when, drawing from Buddhist wisdom, she shared her life assumption that everyone she meets is, in their own way, fighting a mighty battle.

There are also many thoughts which seem to be completely at odds with the celebrated individuals who propose them. 'Movement is tranquillity', the guiding thought of motor-racing legend Sir Stirling Moss, initially seems a bizarre notion from a man famous for hurtling around a track at neck-snapping velocity. So too award-winning Japanese architect Dr Kisho Kurokawa advocates nothing in terms of structure, form, or function, but a greater philosophy of symbiosis. Professor Grahame Webb, a clear-headed leader in the field of wildlife conservation, engages not with the destruction of the environment but with the abolition of poverty.

Unleashing the devastating power of the atom serves as a timeless reminder of the awesome potential that lies dormant in the heart of even the smallest being. It is right that we should seek this out in ourselves and direct its purpose to that which would bring us and those we love the greatest happiness.

Bradley Trevor Greive

VIRGINIA MCKENNA

British actress and animal conservationist

The happiness and fulfilment I have enjoyed from a long and happy marriage to Bill Travers and my family life with four children and seven grandchildren is difficult to explain in a few words, but perhaps our close affinity was increased by our thoughts, concerns and feelings about nature and wild animals. Especially about wild animals in captivity, which are isolated from nature and are, accordingly, deprived of a natural way of life.

Our interest began in 1964 during the filming of *Born Free*, and became a passion. In 1984, together with our son Will, we started Zoo Check—since 1991 renamed the Born Free Foundation. Through this work I have a wonderful chance to put something back into life and, hopefully, to influence people to regard animals in a kinder and more sensitive way.

SIR RANULPH FIENNES

British adventurer

Try chewing a few prawns before you announce to the world that you intend to devour an entire lobster.

MAEVE BINCHY

Irish author

You can't be bored with people if you know their life stories. The dullest soul is interesting if you can tell what events shaped their lives. Maybe they had great teachers, false friends, selfish spouses, depressing work conditions.

I have learned to look into the face of every stranger as if it were a canvas. It's been very useful to me in my trade of storytelling since I'm never short of a plot, but I like to think it has been helpful too in making me more understanding about my fellow humans while we are here on this planet.

DR JOSE RAMOS-HORTA

Nobel Peace Prize Laureate, East Timor

Throughout history, demagogues, the false prophets and tyrants saw their empires, built on falsehoods, arrogance and force, crumble like a castle of cards. In the face of fanatacism and intolerance we must not despair nor lose faith, must not give up our quest for freedom and human dignity, for we shall prevail.

An impossible dream can be realised if we stay focused with serenity and determination, never debasing ourselves with hatred and violence against those who call us their enemy.

NANCY-BIRD WALTON, AO, OBE

Australian aviatrix

My passion—and purpose in life at an early age—was to learn to fly. Once I had achieved that goal, my passion then was to inspire other women to fly. It is wonderful to know that now there are over fifty women on the flight deck of Qantas (from second officers to captains), two in the Royal Australian Navy, six in the Australian Army (including flying Blackhawk helicopters) and ten in the Royal Australian Air Force flying everything from Hercules to F-111s.

My sense of purpose during my flying years was to help the Sydney Far West Children's Health Scheme, now the Royal Far West Children's Health Scheme, and also services for the aged, to fly a medical baby clinic—and provide an air ambulance in an emergency—to look after the health of isolated children in the outback of New South Wales.

GARRY KASPAROV

Russian-Armenian, ranked world's number one chess player

I never tackle anything half-heartedly. If it's worth doing, it's worth doing properly.

SIR GUSTAV NOSSAL,
AC, CBE, FAA, FRS

Professor Emeritus, University of Melbourne

I feel my work makes use of the knowledge and experience that I gathered over my research career and hopefully pays something back to society for the quite wonderful experience that I had of following my dream of medical research for so many years. Although my work was very much at the basic, fundamental science end of the spectrum, I always felt that the longer term implications of the work could have practical impacts on human health.

WILLIAM DALRYMPLE

British author

Always remember there are many roads up the mountain.

JEFFREY MASSON, PhD

American author

For years I was a controversial psychoanalyst, or at least a psychoanalyst involved in controversial issues. But I had the terrible feeling that I was missing something essential. For a long time I thought the deepest thoughts were about the deepest sorrows. I may have been right, but for the last fifteen years I have moved away from human misery to gaze with awe, admiration and humility into the emotional eyes of animals.

Their world of feeling is taking me into areas of thought I never believed I would visit. I am not a spiritual man, and I have learned to avoid all human gurus, but now it occurs to me that animals who live in the moment and whose ability to fully sense the joy in that moment, are, or could be, our true teachers.

We have always admired animals for their ability to do physical things we cannot—fly in the air, swim fast in the ocean, run immense distances at great speed—but now I admire the fact that so many animals seem to have access to deep feelings and that these emotions are purer and perhaps more intense than anything we—or at least I—feel.

I like the profound feeling of humility that admiration induces in me, not to mention that I will never eat any animal ever again. How do you put into your mouth a being who feels more deeply than you do?

PETER SINGER

*DeCamp Professor of Bioethics,
University Center for Human Values, Princeton University*

Try to live your life so that the world has been a better place because you lived in it. And if you are in doubt about what makes the world better, then start by doing something to reduce the vast quantity of pointless pain and suffering present on this planet.

HELEN GURLEY BROWN

Editor-In-Chief, International Editions Cosmopolitan magazine

I think one's priority in life is just to get up and do the best you can every day. That sounds a little clichéd and unimaginative, but we know gruesome things happen to all of us and have to be gotten through. But we also know—or at least I know, having had it happen to me—that if you really try, just get up and do the drudgery, give the job, even the one you are not crazy about, everything you've got, you are probably going to wind up okay.

GENERAL PETER COSGROVE, AC, MC

Chief of the Australian Defence Force

My life has been all about leadership. My first test of real leadership came at the age of twenty-two when fighting in Vietnam. I was responsible for the lives and wellbeing of thirty young Australians, an infantry platoon of soldiers. Despite all my training, the stark actuality of being a leader, making life-and-death decisions, was very confronting. Since that time, an acute awareness of the privilege and responsibility inherent in leading others has remained with me always. It is the aspect of my life that gives me the greatest satisfaction, at the pinnacle of my military career, as I consider the safety and wellbeing of our people who are daily in harm's way.

Leadership is essential, not only in my career but in all walks of life. Leadership is about people, focusing their efforts as a team— its essence is integrity of character. Given time and experience, most qualities can be acquired or developed to a reasonable standard. The exception to this rule is the priceless commodity of integrity.

Belief in your integrity—as distinct from popularity—is what binds people to your ideas and vision. With a team working as one, the impossible can be achieved.

PAYZA DORJI

Trekking and culture guide, Bhutan

Bhutan is a deeply spiritual, landlocked country and we treasure our unique and rich cultural heritage. As profound devotees of Buddhism we feel that the modern development of machines and weapons does not necessarily make people happy or free them from misery. These things may provide temporary satisfaction but as human beings, our wants and needs are unlimited due to our insatiable egos. Instead, we should focus on our inner qualities. We need to cultivate deep human compassion, love and respect for others.

For me it is beautiful to see the setting rays of the sun gradually vanishing from the tips of our sacred Jhomolhari mountain. In the Paro valley we are blessed with blue sky and clean and green surroundings. There are groups of prayer flags on every hilltop and marvellous views of temples, monasteries and hermitages in every corner of the landscape.

We have a religious saying in Bhutan: 'Look at the present physical and mental condition to learn what deeds were done in the past life. Look at one's present deeds to know what one will do in the next life.'

ROLF HARRIS, OBE, AM

UK-based Australian entertainer

The best and most telling bit of advice I ever heard was from an elderly man who put out classical CDs and LPs of fairly obscure works. He had become obsessed with classical music from the age of four, when he listened to his grandmother's record collection. As soon as he was able, he steered his life towards classical music, and eventually ended up with his own small label, doing what he had always wanted to do, spreading his enthusiasm for classical music to the world.

He was being honoured for his lifetime's work by the music industry, and in his acceptance speech he said, 'When I was thirteen, a friend of my father's gave me this telling and life-changing piece of advice, and I pass it on freely: "First identify your obsession. Then make it your profession, and you will never do another day's work in your life!" I proceeded to do just that, and I would recommend it to everyone.'

As I listened to him, I realised that is exactly what I had been doing all my own life.

Try to make your hobby your life's work!

DAN MILLMAN

*American former world trampoline champion,
Stanford University gymnastics coach, Oberlin College professor and author*

After traversing life's winding paths for nearly six decades, I've found four sorts of purposes common to us all.

We're here to learn—Earth is a school and daily life is our classroom. Daily life is guaranteed to teach us everything we need to learn in order to evolve. Challenges in the arenas of health, relationships, finances and career all test us, temper us, and reveal us to ourselves. Every choice leads to wisdom.

We're here to serve—to do whatever we do to the best of our ability. No occupation is more spiritual than any other; spirit is what we bring to our work. Whether we call it a profession, career, calling, or just a job, our form of service connects us with others as we contribute to the common good.

We're here to mature through our life path—one of thirty-seven outlined in my book, *The Life You Were Born to Live*, which pinpoints the challenges and capacities on each path and the laws to transcend them.

We are here to live moment-to-moment—each moment brings a task, a challenge, a goal. It's good to have big goals, but we need to connect the dots between where we are and where we're going, one day, one moment, at a time.

BARRY CROCKER

Australian entertainer and author

As a young and callow fellow I followed colour and movement with absolute passion; the colours could never be bright enough or the movement too fast. But now, realising I've almost straddled life's obstacle course, I find pastel shades and unhurried journeys permeate my thoughts. Approaching the climax of my odyssey, I've learned that fame and fortune, no matter how great, have not provided me with inner peace.

Inner peace lifts you to the pinnacle of existence, but to attain this you must first slay your dragons. I have glimpses of this tranquil euphoric state, but how to make it permanent? Aye, there lies the rub.

WILL CARLING, OBE

British rugby star and sports commentator

The most fulfilling experience in my life has been with my family—the sheer pleasure of being alongside my wife, while trying to guide and encourage our children. It is hard to express the joy found in watching them grow, watching them learn and laugh.

There can be nothing more important than nurturing your children and passing on to them the importance of others, the importance of living your life by the right principles and enjoying it all before it has gone.

DR ROBERT D. BALLARD

American oceanographer, President of the Institute for Exploration, and led and participated in more than 100 deep-sea expeditions, including discovery of the ships Titanic, Bismarck and Lusitania

I was taught by my mid-western parents and grandmother to 'Leave it better than you found it'. That simple saying goes a long way in life, whether it is cleaning a room as you walk through or doing great deeds that have a positive impact upon the world. I was also taught to 'Never get into the thick of thin things'. When you pick something in life to do, pick something big.

DERRYN HINCH

Author and radio broadcaster, Melbourne

As a journalist, editor and foreign correspondent, I have interviewed many stellar performers around the world during a media career of forty-five years. My message is maybe more simple than most. I yearn to have only two words on my tombstone: 'He tried.'

Tried to make this place a better one than when I entered it. Tried to make males less chauvinistic. Tried, through the mediums of newspapers and radio and television, to make people more genuinely tolerant towards each other on the issues of race and colour and religion. And I am an atheist.

My most telling achievement—and message—was going to jail for contempt of court because I exposed a paedophile priest running a youth camp when he already had served time for child rape. And through it all I remembered the sobering Irish dictum: 'The longer you live, the sooner you die.'

I tried. I did.

BRADLEY TREVOR GREIVE

Author of The Blue Day Book and Priceless: The Vanishing Beauty of a Fragile Planet, conservationist and Governor of the Taronga Foundation, Tasmania (www.tarongafoundation.com)

In my heart I am an explorer. It may seem perverse for someone who spends so much time in pyjamas to make such a claim, but there it is.

Like you, I drew my first breath on a planet already covered in tyre tracks and footprints, so perhaps you may wonder what it matters to be an explorer in this day and age. My dear friend, it matters—it matters to me.

We cannot go back in time to see what was, but we can go to the edge of the world to see what is. I have stood beneath a whirlwind of crimson dragonflies in the hills of Luzon and been startled by the frigid gasp of an elephant seal surfacing in the icy waters off Vancouver Island. I have swayed beneath the emerald ceiling of a Thai rainforest on the back of an elephant and had a fresh fig lovingly massaged into my hair by a black-and-white ruffed lemur. I have waited at dawn on a small Pacific atoll and watched baby sea-turtles hatch, exploding out of the sand and tumbling down the beach into the ocean like happy leather buttons.

Every time I discover something new it is as if I have unearthed another tiny, precious piece of myself. Although their numbers are falling by the hour, there are still over one million species of plants and animals that breathe the same air and embrace the earth as we do. To see them is to know them, to know them is to love them.

I will see them all or die trying.

PROFESSOR ALLAN SNYDER, FRS

Director of Centre for the Mind, a joint venture between the Australian National University, Canberra, and the University of Sydney

I strive to pour something uniquely me into everything. Ultimately, I work towards a contribution that changes how people think and enriches humankind. This passionate pursuit is a joy!

SUE FEAR

*Second Australian woman to summit Mount Everest
and the first to do so from Tibet, and Australian Adventurer of the Year 2003*

My life as a climber and work as a guide in remote and beautiful natural places is very fulfilling. Mountains always present a challenge. When I guide others, I know that together we can meet these challenges and overcome them. I like to empower others, to energise and inspire them. I know that together we can climb the mountain, or work together to make the world a better place.

My lightweight style of mountaineering, a kind of minimalist approach to climbing, has developed into an attitude about life in general. It's about keeping your eye on the main game and not losing sight of what's most important, knowing that you can take in small ways, but give back as well. Like everything, it's a balancing act.

The mountains nurture my spirit—a spirit for life that cannot easily be crushed.

DI MORRISSEY

Australian author

It's not often we take a step to one side and actually look at life. When I took control of my own destiny a number of years ago—by taking the plunge to fulfil my childhood dream of writing books—I came to the conclusion I should take that step and reflect on where I was in my life's journey.

I was on my own for the first time in my life, divorced, my kids studying overseas. I had to manage my life myself, from getting a carpet snake out of the bedroom, rescuing chickens from the fox, and fixing the house and garden, to struggling financially and trying to finish my first novel.

But I found moments of great joy every day. The appreciation of my environment enriched my life. If I felt frustrated or miserable, I stepped outside the door and said to myself, 'Stop whingeing. Look at where you live.' I was renting a small cabin far from neighbours and surrounded by bush, and nearby the sound of the ocean reminded me it was time to walk the dog on the beach.

I dreamed of being a successful author, of making money, finding a mate. Then one day I realised what was really important in life: family, knowing my kids were healthy and happy, watching sea hawks swoop, the golden shadows of evening lengthening to twilight. I had the sense that all would be alright. And it was. And is.

THE HON. TIM FISCHER

Former Australian Deputy Prime Minister

'Worthwhile' is a wonderful concept, a very positive description of certain activities. I have been fortunate to have had a diverse life of tasks large and small, activities with headlines and at other times a long way from headlines, all beginning at a small place called Boree Creek in mid-outback Australia, where I grew up in a large family.

What has made it especially worthwhile has been on good days and bad days, I always looked for the opportunity to reach out and give a hand up or a positive greeting to someone not expecting recognition and often a long way out from the inner circle.

In my early days I received some worthwhile help and a useful hand up, often unexpected. My life is the richer for endeavouring to reciprocate now I can give something back in this post-parliamentary phase of my life. Whilst the 'Me, must have now' generation dominates today, they are ultimately diminished by not knowing of the joy from helping others, even when helping on a modest scale.

So being a sensible, practical but admittedly less than perfect Samaritan makes my life worthwhile, from my own young family to interesting people and projects in the Great Outback, and not to forget the tiny kingdom of Bhutan for the 'Heaven' of it all!

RAMON BLANCO

Spanish-Venezuelan luthier and mountaineer who has climbed the highest peaks on seven continents, including Everest at the age of sixty

It was not my intention to be a mountaineer. However, when I was thirty, I climbed Popocatepetl, a dormant volcano in Mexico. As I ascended I was gripped by the grandeur of the nature I was passing through. I was brought to tears by the intense silence at the rim of the crater. This holds a permanent place in my mind. It transformed me from being a lowlander into a mountaineer. I learned that immersion in a pristine natural environment gives a deep sense of fulfilment which cannot be experienced for me in an urban environment.

Many years passed. I climbed other mountains and I also explored the jungles. I was captivated by the diversity of these environments. Now I see them as a metaphor for the human condition, at times erupting like the Sangay volcano in Ecuador and at other times serene and harmonious like the jungles of Venezuela.

For me, the purpose of life is to strive for inner peace. The effort of extreme physical achievement is a catalyst for this state of mind.

PETER GARRETT, AM

*President of the Australian Conservation Foundation, activist,
former member Australian group Midnight Oil*

I have a deep feeling that to love; that is, to try and give freely, to listen without judgment, to care for those around us and beyond—including the living world—is the most important human impulse.

While I often fall short of expressing this kind of love, I'm convinced that it is fundamental to our wellbeing and to human survival. It is right to live a loving life, one that has a purpose which includes aiming to do good where we discern good can be done and then acting decisively and with the full engagement of our capacities to make it come about.

I also need to reflect on the transcendent, and the faithful lives lived, including that of Jesus Christ, to make my way surer in a hurried and crowded world where narcissism and selfishness abound.

I believe that love given in this way is the most challenging yet the most important of our actions and the more we can aim for it, the better off our lives and the lives of all our neighbours will be.

RICHARD WOOLCOTT, AC

Former Secretary of the Department of Foreign Affairs and Trade and former Australian Ambassador to the United Nations, Indonesia and the Philippines

Australia is a work in progress. After forty years in the Foreign Service and having travelled throughout this vast continent and represented Australia overseas, I love this country. I want it to achieve its full potential. In this context I have had five major and related priorities which, in the twilight of my life, I am still pursuing.

They are the successful consolidation of a fair, tolerant, non-racist, multi-ethnic Australian democracy; the establishment of a distinctly Australian republic; with its own head of state, that has severed its anachronistic links with the English crown; the achievement of genuine reconciliation between immigrant Australians and the indigenous peoples they dispossessed; the full emergence of an Australia, comfortably and constructively engaged with—and accepted as a partner by—the countries of the region in which we live; and, more recently, the restoration of truth and accountability to the conduct of our government.

Priority for the family is also important to me. The family is the life raft that takes us from one generation to the next. All my family have enriched my life in different ways. I hope our grandchildren will live in a more peaceful, safer and just world than my generation.

DEBORAH TABART

Executive Director, Australian Koala Foundation

Now that I am fifty plus I am enjoying the freedom of knowing that I know…well, that I know some things.

I know that courage and freedom of speech are imperative for the human spirit. I know that every human being and animal has a spiritual purpose here on earth. This is of great support to me and gives meaning to my journey of life. I know that our cruelty towards human beings and animals is wrong. I know that we must seek to find compassion and love in ourselves first and then spread it outwards. I know how impossibly hard that can be. I know that family and friends are our saviours in times of turmoil, and that some family and friends are the reason for that turmoil in the first place. I know the agony and the ecstasy of death and birth. I also know, luckily, how it feels when you see a mother koala and her joey sleeping peacefully high in the treetops, safe in the wild.

BRUCE RUXTON, AM, OBE

Former President of the Australian Returned Servicemen's League, Queensland

We have all heard the phrase 'to have a purpose in life'. Not many people have a purposeful life and that is unfortunate. My purpose in life has been to ensure governments keep their promises to the Veteran community, which means, of course, that the politicians have to be watched continually to see those promises are not broken. Fulfilment in life is a purposeful life, and a grand purpose in life is to be able to look after people less fortunate—the sick, the homeless and the elderly.

If you are bored with life, correct your thinking—and do something worthwhile.

SHASHI DESHPANDE

Indian novelist

Through writing, which has made my life rich and meaningful, I have tried to understand humans. I find us—our endless variations, our essential sameness, our strengths, our frailties, our overwhelming desire to live, our anguish at what life offers us and above all, our relationships with one another—endlessly fascinating. In each novel I explore these things, asking questions, rarely having the answers, but finding that the questions themselves bring in a little more light. Each novel is a voyage of discovery for me, a discovery of myself, of other humans, of our universe. There never has been any huge enlightenment, only an understanding of the fact that as we live, we learn to cope, becoming each day a little more understanding of human frailty, a little more compassionate. Knowing that if we can't do this, we're sunk, because humans have nothing else, no one else, but themselves. Writing is for me part of the endeavour to understand this process, to articulate the human struggle, the human triumph. If I am able to help even one reader find this understanding, it makes my work worthwhile.

ROBERT E. KOWALSKI

Medical writer, lecturer and consultant, California

If a magical 'financial fairy godmother' came along and offered you a choice between financial ruin and bankruptcy or financial fortune, I can't imagine that you'd pick the former. Everyone would like to be wealthy. Riches are better than rags.

In a very real way, everyone can make the same choice between vibrant good health and longevity and illness and disease. Sadly, most men and women make the wrong choices. Here's an investment planner that really pays off in both short-term and long-term health dividends.

The first two are truly no-brainers: fasten your seatbelt every time you're in a car, and quit smoking. Both will add years of life. Next, as Hippocrates first said in far more eloquent words: use it or lose it. That is, keep physically active. Do what you enjoy. Walk, hike, bike, swim, dance, jog, garden—you name it. Just get your heart beating rapidly at least thirty minutes a day.

Sure, you've heard it all before. Just like you've heard about wise financial investments. Don't wait to make these health investments.

TIM COSTELLO

Chief Executive Officer, World Vision, Australia

'Mistakes aren't shameful.' I make this emphasis wherever and whenever I can in order to counterbalance the overwhelming message rife in our society that communicates a sense of failure and the dreadful stigma of being a 'loser'.

Making errors and admitting to them, letting ourselves be vulnerable to honest feedback that might expose our mistakes, and not being ashamed of our brokenness, are all part of the Christian doctrine of forgiveness. If lived out and expressed in the community, it is the most healing force I know.

LADY MARY FAIRFAX, AM, OBE

Australian philanthropist

Touch every life with good.

DR JUDITH BLACKSHAW

Former Professor of Veterinarian Medicine, University of Queensland

The time had come to downsize our possessions as we were preparing to sell our house and move to a townhouse. The first task was to sort out our pictures and decide what would fit into the new house.

The family photographs could be safely put in an album, but what about the picture of the bushranger? Probably not an art critic's choice, this picture means a lot to us. When our son was sixteen years old he travelled 2000 kilometres to be trained as a jackaroo on a large sheep property. The first six months were difficult for him as the overseer was an unpleasant man to all the young jackaroos. One by one they left. Our son rang us in great distress and said he wanted to leave too.

My heart went out to him, but I talked with him about how sometimes things in life are difficult and we have to learn to cope. Also the shearing season was coming up and it would be difficult for the station owner if everyone left. Our son stayed and helped with the frantic shearing season.

At the end of this period, the station owner thanked him for staying, fired the overseer and gave our son a double pay-rise. That Christmas, our son bought us the bushranger picture for our present. That was twenty-three years ago and we treasure the picture and also the responsible, considerate person our son is to his family and the people he works with.

Gifts such as these are beyond price. They are the precious parts of our lives—the cards your daughter makes for your birthday, the pictures and paper chains your grandson and his sister made for Christmas decorations. These are gifts we keep forever—in our hearts.

RT REV. RICHARD HARRIES

Bishop of Oxford

A prayer in the letter to Ephesians contains the words, 'With deep roots and firm foundations may you, in company with all God's people, be strong to grasp what is the breadth and length and height and depth of Christ's love, and to know it, though it is beyond knowledge. So may you be filled with the very fullness of God.'

What an extraordinary thought—that frail, fallible mortals like us are to be filled with the divine life. I don't think you have to be a Christian to see this. Nelson Mandela wrote, 'We were born to make manifest the glory of God that is within us. It is not just in some of us; it is in everyone.'

For me, those words sum up where, above all, we find purpose and meaning in our life.

ALFRED GREGORY

Climbing member and official stills photographer of the triumphant 1953 Everest team, Himalayan explorer and professional photographer, Melbourne

The things which most affect one's life are often those that just happen, but more likely, they will be the things you make happen. In my life I have been lucky to have lived at a time when much of the mountain world was still completely unknown and unmapped. So I went there.

The world out there is waiting for you. Pack your rucksack and just go. It's dangerous, of course—so what? To have lived a life without danger is not to have lived at all.

ZITA WEBER

Australian academic and author

It has been said that we are born into stories. But more importantly, we are all story-makers. We make and remake the story of our own life. We have our dominant stories, which we are currently living out, and we have our alternative stories, those that lie just beneath the surface. We can change our story to make a difference in our lives.

I remember the day I became aware of the power to make a difference, and that differences matter. I was working with children at risk, whose dominant life story was one of danger and uncertainty, whose pasts had damaged them and whose futures were fragile. I was also working with mothers who had dominant stories of anger and abuse—a sense of powerlessness and self-esteem so low that only violence assuaged their damaged egos.

I was in court when I realised for the first time how our stories, our narratives can come to constrict us, or free us, depending on our choices. Our lives are not set in stone. Finding out how we might live differently can be confronting. And emotionally life-saving. Differences do matter.

BRIAN ALDISS

British writer and critic

During World War II, we observed a strict blackout in England which had the advantage of there usually being clear viewings of the starry heavens. As a small boy I used to imagine civilised worlds up there, with cultured and peaceable people travelling in great ships from one world to another, to share their wisdom and experience. I no longer believe this scenario, although I wish it were so. The universe at large is not a particularly friendly place for biological entities.

The best that we can do in life is not to be fanatical, not to indulge in hatred, and to be, as far as we can, always good humoured and optimistic: that is to say, to hope for the best while fearing the worst. And while we behave as badly as we do, we should remain within the confines of our own solar system.

VERONICA BRADY

Retired academic and Roman Catholic nun, Western Australia

I discovered the purpose of life, I think, as a child one sunny morning in our backyard. Lying under the lemon tree in bloom, my legs in the warm sunshine with the rest of me in the scented shade, I knew myself as part of the large and mysterious whole of life, what Dante called, the 'great ocean of being' across which all living things move and always have moved, some in joy, some in pain, but each borne to its own destination.

What I have to do, therefore, is to be who I am and be aware of myself as part of this community, caring for it, loving and respecting but above all practising it. The German poet Rilke put it this way:

> *... Are we perhaps, here, only to say: House.*
> *Bridge. Fountain. Gate. Jug. Fruit-tree. Window—*
> *at most: Pillar. Tower ... But to say, you understand,*
> *O to say, with an intensity the things themselves never*
> *Hoped to achieve.*

DR FERID MURAD, MD, PhD

American Professor of Pharmacology, Nobel Laureate in Medicine or Physiology

In spite of coming from a poor middle-class family with very little education, as a youngster I was determined to become a physician and scientist. With such determination, hard work, many jobs, and the ability to obtain several scholarships, I succeeded in obtaining excellent training in medicine, pharmacology and biochemistry.

I have been blessed with a wonderful wife, five children and nine grandchildren who have permitted me to focus on my love for research. My research has and will continue to influence the lives of millions of people. There can be no greater gift and reward. If only I could once again discover something as important that could help many more.

DR JOHN YU, AC

Chancellor, University of New South Wales

The world will be a better place if children are given our first priority when it comes to the distribution of governmental resources, not just our children but all children, especially those in disadvantaged communities.

CAPTAIN M.S. KOHLI

Mountaineer and author, India

Right from my childhood, I firmly believed that apart from individual achievements, one should do something for society for a more meaningful life.

I feel a great sense of satisfaction for conceiving and promoting trekking in the Himalayas in 1971 by touring over fifty countries, and as President of the Indian Mountaineering Foundation, introducing a number of landmark developments. I found a sense of great purpose in founding the Himalayan Environment Trust in 1989 with some of the world's living legends as trustees: Sir Edmund Hillary, Sir Chris Bonington, Reinhold Messner, Maurice Herzog and Junko Tabei.

But what gave me the highest satisfaction in life is my recent book about the power of prayer, which describes divine experiences and miraculous instances of survival in my life. The entire royalty from this book goes to an Indian charity, Pingalwara, which is doing wonderful work for the disabled and mentally challenged.

DORIS BRETT

Psychologist, author and poet, Melbourne

In all the hundreds of exams, tests, questionnaires, data-collecting surveys and the multitude of quizzes that we have been subject to by the time we reach our adult years, no one has ever asked us, 'What is the purpose of your life? What gives your life meaning?' And yet surely, these are the most important questions we will ever consider.

Love has to be first. The people I love, my family, my friends, the people who love me. Without those, I would be bereft. Justice, learning, beauty, diversity, wit, courage, integrity all come tumbling through. Words that barely require explanation, yet are all important to me. And in amongst them, another shaping force—the sense of wanting to be of service in a way that reaches beyond my own personal circle. I grew up aware of how privileged I was—two parents who loved me, material comfort, a lucky country. I have always felt that it is important to give back, to reach out, to make a meaningful difference.

LADY POTTER, AC

Philanthropist and charity worker, Melbourne

Two things amongst many stand out for me. First, seeing a young child who was born profoundly deaf, hearing for the first time after receiving a cochlear implant—the look of wonder and joy on her face was unforgettable! I think the same look of joy and wonder was on my face when I first held my ten-minute-old granddaughter, the greatest blessing imaginable.

BRUCE SMEATON

Australian composer

Composing has never been easy. Even Mozart wrote to his father about his difficulties, while Beethoven's agonising is legendary. Knowing what you want to do is one thing, but the towering achievements of the past can be both inspirational and daunting.

About fifty years ago I was, by chance, invited to a very swish party in Melbourne. My hostess looked me up and down as if I had just crawled out of a sewer. 'So, you're the young man who is *supposed* to be a composer? Well, you can take yourself off to the piano and compose something.' She had a face like a dropped meat pie, if that's helpful.

I went to the piano taking a very big problem with me—I was a woodwind player, not a pianist. Nevertheless, I thought for a minute and began to play. Within thirty seconds she put her face close to my ear and hissed, 'That's not composing. You're just making that up!'

The old battleaxe had hit the right button. It released the blocks and I've never stopped making music from that moment to this. Encourage young people. It costs nothing and they are the only future we've got.

ONG KIM SENG

Internationally renowned watercolourist, Singapore

As a watercolourist I preserve scenes from nature, and wish that I could retard the pace of development which can be so destructive.

I enjoy witnessing daybreak, the switching off of streetlights, the waking up of birds in the trees, and the neighbour's children setting off for school. I say to myself it is the start of another day, never to return. Use it wisely.

THE HON. DEE MARGETTS, MLC

Australian politician, member of the Greens party

In the mid to late 1970s, while studying part-time for a BA double-major at the University of Western Australia, I was quite despondent about the state of the world. I had read a number of publications that appeared to point to an inevitable depletion of the world's non-renewable resources. I found myself choosing courses in Development Studies and began reading J.K. Galbraith and Susan George. It was like the scales had dropped away from my eyes.

I began to realise it was not the world's teeming millions who were inevitably consuming the world's precious resources, but that the smallest, richest portion of the world's population were controlling and using the world's resources in an unsustainable manner. I travelled to England, where I subsequently completed an honours degree in Development Studies at the University of East Anglia.

This background has given me the ability to stand back and see my own country's economy and society far more clearly. In the Australian Senate and now as a regional Western Australian parliamentarian, one of my main driving passions has been to bring some commonsense to the debate in Australia and my own state around the process of corporate globalisation.

ANTONY NICHOLAS

Executive Director of People Living with HIV/AIDS (NSW), Australia

Having spent much of my childhood holidays with my nana, I was lucky enough to discover some of her ancient wisdom: a love of beautiful things, family and friends, and importantly, a concern for human frailty and troubled lives. In her eighties she was still cooking meals for the 'old dears'—many younger than herself—who needed help. Such optimism and sense of duty about our true place in the world was one of her greatest offerings to me, an inspiration that still touches me decades later.

Working with people living with HIV, I am frequently asked if it's depressing. I always answer 'inspiring'. To be part of everyday human triumph, in everyday lives, responding to extraordinary circumstances, often with high spirits, with caring and a smile. I always think I am lucky to have these experiences, to have known ordinary people living extraordinary lives. Nevertheless, it reminds me to reflect that life is uncertain and can change spectacularly in an instant. It's a cliché, I know, but life is too short for rehearsals.

FATHER TIMOTHY RADCLIFFE, OP

Former Master of the Order of Preachers (The Dominicans) Blackfriars, Oxford

Yesterday I received an email from a young Egyptian Muslim whom I met in Cairo last year. He is studying to be an Imam, and he is called Amir. We keep in touch out of friendship, and in the hope that Christians and Muslims and Jews may grow in friendship rather than tear each other to pieces. All my life I have been deeply moved by unexpected friendships with strangers, people of other cultures and faiths. As a Christian I believe that each of these friendships is the promise of more, that friendship is the very life of God and where all humanity will find its home.

DR JEROME KARLE

Nobel Laureate in Chemistry, Washington, DC

Two words that are important to me are honesty and respect. The opposite of the concepts generated by those words, dishonesty and disrespect, have led to great suffering in the history of man. The very large numbers of people whose motivations are money and power, are a danger to themselves and the societies in which they live.

There is a real danger that the destructive aspects of money and power, and the disrespect for human life, will cause great difficulty in the not too distant future. Consider, for example, how undesirable motivations have interfered with proper attention to global warming, the disappearance of energy resources, of farmland and of forests, pollution of the earth and the oceans and the spread of deadly diseases. When does the point of no return enter, or has it?

VAL GROGAN, AM

President of St John Ambulance (NSW), Australia

My Christian faith has been the motivating force in my life. I do not believe that we are here on Earth by accident. Christ's example is one of service to others and concern for the needy and disadvantaged. I have tried to put these principles into practice in my daily life and through voluntary work in a number of organisations and charities, including St John Ambulance Australia and the Society of the Friends of St George's Chapel, Windsor Castle, in the United Kingdom.

I have also been involved with rule of law and human rights issues, in particular relating to Tibet. A highlight of my life was staying in a Tibetan refugee settlement in Sikkim in 1968, when I was asked to form a branch of the Tibetan Friendship Group in Australia. Another highlight was an audience with His Holiness the Dalai Lama in Dharamsala in 1975, when we formed the Australian Tibetan Society with His Holiness as patron. The Dalai Lama's compassion, humility, sense of humour and peaceful concern for justice has been an inspiration to me in my ongoing involvement with the Tibetan people and their cause.

DR NICHOLAS COLEMAN

World Religions Consultant, Wesley College, Elsternwick Campus, Melbourne

Religious educators are fair game for tough questions. A young freckled-faced student approached me in the crowded courtyard one sunny winter's afternoon and, chuckling mischievously, asked me, 'Hey, Doc, what's the meaning of life?'

My gaze took in the moment—the boy, the other students, school buildings and a huge tree nearby. My eyes travelled up the leafless tree, seeing how its trunk divided into mighty limbs which spread into big branches that separated into smaller boughs, then parted into a thicket of stems and finally reached thousands of slender twigs towards the sky like fingers in silent prayer to the warm sun and life itself. As I began to describe the magic of meaning in nature, the student quickly interrupted, 'No, no, Doc. I mean, what's the meaning of life?'

'Ah,' I said, lowering my gaze to the boy's level. 'Well, the meaning of life is like the taste of an orange. There's only one way to know that taste, and that is…'

'To get an orange and eat it?' the lad suggested tentatively.

'Correct,' I replied. 'And there's only one way to really know the meaning of life.'

'You mean, get a life and live it?' said the twelve-year-old, speaking slowly now, wondering at his own words.

'Indeed,' I agreed heartily. 'To know the meaning of life, we need to get a life and live it!'

We parted then, with both our lives made a little more meaningful.

ARNOLD WESKER

British playwright and director

I care passionately about my children, grandchildren, and now a great-grandchild. All I want is that more and more of my work should be performed and published so that I can leave them all something to steady them against the mistakes they will make and life's vicissitudes.

And all that I care about humanity is there in my writings. Thus, the more the work is performed the more both might benefit—my family and humanity.

TIM AND PAULINE CARR

The only permanent inhabitants of South Georgia Island, South Atlantic, renowned blue water sailors and curators of the South Georgia Museum

There can be no conquering of mountains or mastery of oceans. We ride on nature's shoulder only as long as we are not a burden. It is better to leave no tracks, no signs of man's passing and our wake soon melts back into the waves.

ARCHIE BIGG

Poet, Norfolk Island, South Pacific, sixth generation descendant of the Bounty mutineers Fletcher Christian and Matthew Quintal, and their Tahitian wives Mauatua and Tevarua

To be fortunate enough to experience the love and support of a family such as mine makes me feel so very privileged, and to foster in the young members of our Norfolk Island 'Bounty' family a knowledge of their culture and heritage gives me great pride and satisfaction.

KEN ANNAKIN, OBE, DLit

British film director and author

My life has been made worthwhile by contact with people of all nationalities and classes—first as a hobo in New Zealand and Australia, then as a film-maker in many parts of the world. That, and Pauline my wonderful wife of forty-four years, have made me the luckiest man in the world. In return, I have always made the effort to give advice and good ideas to young people who need encouragement to be adventurous and creative.

PROFESSOR RICHARD GREEN

Classical archaeologist, University of Sydney

What has inspired me through the years is, I suppose, an abiding curiosity about the ancient world and a desire to see what made the Greeks like us but different from us, and how it was they were such a dynamic group of people who set Western civilisation on its track.

My research has covered many areas in Greek and Roman archaeology, but over more recent years I have concentrated on how the Greeks represented themselves in the theatre and, in as much as theatre is a mirror of life, what that can tell us of the way they viewed themselves.

In the end, knowledge of other cultures can give us a better view of ourselves and our place in the world, and, one would hope, teach us that humankind has more than petty nationalisms and selfish attitudes.

RENEE GOOSSENS

Australian author

Let us not be weighed down in sorrow or hopelessness by the immense problems of the world. Changing our focus may well be the most important lesson of life. Ease the pain of others, be aware of access problems for those with mobility restrictions and assist them with discretion and gentleness. Do not presume to judge, remembering that our perceived infallibility is as dangerous as any extremism. Let us instead learn to help those who are antagonistic, to be patient with those whose extreme views cause, both themselves and others, despair, vengeance and to plan the death of others and perhaps drive them to suicidal acts. By personal actions we can do more than hope for a better world.

YOSSI GHINSBERG

Israeli author and adventurer

There is no purpose, but if there was, it would most likely be found in the cessation of its pursuit. The animal kingdom can teach us many things. Jaguars in the forest do not read self-help books, bats in their caves do not pray to gods, the lizards of the desert do not pursue a meaningful existence, the fish in the sea don't look for a cause. Creatures live in the present, never pondering, but are simply connected to the source of life. We search in the wrong place for the wrong thing, not realising that we did not lose anything in the first place.

Stop searching and you may find what you are looking for, or consider that maybe there is nothing to find at all.

ANGUS MCLEOD

Professor Emeritus of Optical Sciences, University of Arizona,
President Thin Film Center Inc, Tucson, Arizona

Both my wife and I had the advantages of a stable upbringing and good education. Our family, love, support and education, have always been uppermost and have shaped virtually everything that we have done. Everything else comes second. It turns out that this is not incompatible with trying to achieve success in a career.

I cannot say that my career has been dominated by any major meaningful goals except that when quite young I decided I wanted to be a physicist. Once on that path, I have simply followed it wherever it took me. I have been very lucky that it has always provided just enough income so that I have never had to face the decision to do something completely different. What I think is most important is the strong support I have had from my wife and our family.

I believe that what I really am is a teacher and, whether I knew it all the time or not, this has directed what I have done in my career.

DENISE LAWUNGKURR GOODFELLOW

Author and illustrator, and member of the Nalangbali clan of the Kunwinjku people of Western Arnhem Land

Many years ago I caught a snake at the request of Gunyok, an Aboriginal elder. To Gunyok it was a test of my resolve to help her people. Putting my life in her hands was my attempt to build trust, for she 'disliked whites'.

She adopted me and my daughter Amber and, as one family, we fought racism and misunderstanding. Following her death, I feared her children and I would lose touch. Then my son, not yet four, was presented with Gunyok's newborn grandson in the Aboriginal way, and the chain continued. Rowan became a responsible adult as Aboriginal children do, by caring for others.

Last year I helped my relatives start The Baby Dreaming Project in Arnhem Land to better fulfil my vow to Gunyok to look after her children. And what have I learned? That the survival of all depends on building bridges, not walls.

DR RICHARD J. ROBERTS

British scientist and research director, Nobel Laureate in Physiology or Medicine

Competition can provide a powerful incentive to succeed and can be a great way to make money and enemies. Collaboration can also lead to success and can promote lifetime friendships, which greatly enrich the quality of one's life. I much prefer collaboration.

HARRY M. MILLER

Celebrity agent and marketing guru, Sydney

I hold to the words about the law of karma from Dadi Janki, spiritual head of the Brahma Kumaris who practises raja yoga: 'Adverse situations will come up in our lives. Instead of being taken by surprise and despairing, we can remain steady and creative. The understanding of predestination is to know that it had to happen. Predestination works hand-in-hand with the philosophy of karma, which reminds us that nothing happens by accident. It also tells us that whatever is happening is good.'

And for me personally, to be just a touch cynical, karma means, 'You can't get away with anything!'

DONALD A. HENDERSON, MD, MPH

Visiting Professor of Medicine and Public Health, Center for Biosecurity,
University of Pittsburgh Medical Center, Baltimore

I was raised in the belief that one's success in life should be measured primarily in terms of the contributions one might make to the betterment of life for one's fellow man—for humanity. That I continue to adhere to this belief may seem old-fashioned and perhaps curious to some, but such successes as I have had in meeting that goal have been, ultimately, the most satisfying.

LINCOLN HALL

Australian mountaineer and author

Life is a gift. You have to unwrap the gift to enjoy it. The problem is that many people think life is a treadmill. And there are those who do see life as a gift, but one so precious they will never unwrap it. These people will never experience its soul-tingling potential.

My teenage son has the opposite approach. He instantly rips the wrapping off presents, and tears apart cereal packets. He rides both himself and his bike to breaking point, sometimes a little past it. His younger brother is more considered in his approach, contemplating all the outcomes before he zooms over a flight of a dozen stairs on his in-line skates.

As a parent I'm torn between worry and delight at this approach to life. I can't admonish them because I'm their role model. Rock climbing was the buzz of my youth, and propelled me on to climbing the biggest mountains in the world. Survival in such places demanded total awareness and the ability to judge myself honestly. Back in the horizontal world, this translates to exploring every little corner of life.

It's an attitude, and my sons are growing to share it with me. My wife had this philosophy when we met, but with different origins, which is why we are so perfect for each other. Her biggest risk was marrying me, knowing that my focus was not secure nest building, knowing that one day I may not return from a mountain. But these days I can value life without surviving difficult mountains. There are safer mountains to climb, more predictable cliffs to scale, and so many people with whom to share the gift of life.

GARY D. BOUMA

Professor of Sociology, Monash University, Melbourne

My life is made meaningful and worthwhile by the continuous practice of the presence of God, the truly transcendent and deeply immanent, through sacrament and meditation. Being suffused with the love of God enables me to be in relationship with others and to seek the good for those people, groups and organisations God gives me to love. The rich diversity of God's love enables and challenges me to accept and affirm those who are both like and very unlike me. When resting in this affirmation I find deep joy and peace. Sharing this reality with my wife makes it all even more beautiful.

SIR FREDERICK HOLLIDAY

British former university vice-chancellor, zoologist and business executive

My priorities are education, education and education.

Without education life is barren; with it, one inhabits two worlds—an outside world and a world inside one's head—both of which are rich and satisfying. To deprive a child of appropriate education is an act of lifelong cruelty.

DR ERIC WOLANSKI, FTSE, FIE

Australian coastal oceanographer

Earlier, I believed that science would be helpful in preserving for our children the spectacular and unique natural heritages such as African wildlife ecosystems and the Great Barrier Reef. I worked with that belief for more than twenty years.

I now hold the view that human forces will destroy most of it within the next few decades, but that a small number of scientists will make a difference and be successful in helping to preserve bits and pieces here and there.

SIR STIRLING MOSS, OBE

British racing car driver

The things that I feel have made my life worthwhile are travel, the people I've met, the cars I've driven and the girls I've loved—and, now, my third wife, who made all the research worthwhile.

Important and meaningful goals are to enjoy life, and try to help others to enjoy it too. My guiding thought is: movement is tranquillity.

CATHERINE DEVRYE

Australian author and former Executive Woman of the Year

When my parents died the year after I graduated from university, I lacked purpose, and promise. I saw no meaning whatsoever in life; at least the life I had always known. An only child, I was unsure how to handle the overwhelming grief, so I rationalised that I had been 'freed' from ordinary parental responsibility to do something extraordinary with my life. So, I set out with a backpack to find a cure for cancer, hunger or conflict in the globe.

With no fixed plan, such lofty ambitions soon gave way to the practicalities of earning a living in the more mundane world of an office environment. I recognised that I was unlikely to fix the big issues but that all of us in our own little way, every day, can still contribute.

Since those early dark days, I've been privileged to meet world leaders, sports stars and music icons and have been surprised to discover that, at times, they all share the same sense of loss and uncertainty as my next-door neighbour or a stranger on a bus, train or plane. No life is perfect and the grass isn't always greener on the other side.

Sure, there have been days of despair but I've always tried to remember what Frank Jansen, a wise old man, told me: 'Cath, every day above the ground is a good one.'

STEPHEN DOWNES

Australian food critic and author

Life has no meaning, to be perfectly objective about it. If we are to believe the scientists—and I do—it is a biological accident. It wasn't designed or intended. Like Topsy, it just grew. Moreover, of all the millions of life forms to have developed, human beings acting in concert and without a sense of universal responsibility are the most despicable.

The great things man stands for—music, paintings, books and thoughts among them—have been achieved almost always by individuals working alone. They took responsibility for confronting our vast potential to commit all manner of acts, both evil and good. They challenged our infinite capacity to damage other things for our own advantage. They realised that in everything we do we are responsible, not just for the effect it has on us but how it might alter any other thing, living or dead.

We are humans, but we are also members of the much bigger groups of life itself and the universe. By accident, we are the only life forms with mature consciences. By responsibility, we should use them.

ROGER MAYNARD

Australian correspondent for the London Times and CNBC Asia

As a journalist I have met more than my share of the haves and have-nots and while I am not a political animal, it really angers me when I see how unfairly people are treated by those who regard themselves as more superior through race, wealth or social standing. Equally, I am infuriated when governments, corporations and individuals try to impose laws and practices which are an affront to personal liberty.

I believe we have to stand up to the politicians, the censors and the spin doctors before we lose many of the freedoms we once took for granted. It is my life's crusade and second only in importance to the love of my family. Nearly thirty years ago I interviewed Barnes Wallis, the scientist who designed the bouncing bomb for the so-called Dambusters, that was to play a crucial role in ending World War II.

Just before he died on the eve of his ninety-second birthday, I asked him what he considered to be his greatest achievement. Without hesitation, the man who had helped to change the course of the war replied, 'My family, of course.'

DR PHILLIP LAW,
AC, CBE, SCTSE, SAA

Australian scientist, Antarctic explorer and educationist

I had no specific ambition as a youth or young man. I wanted to succeed and I determined that each year should result in some advance, professional or personal, such as a higher qualification, a development in sport, learning a new musical instrument, whatever.

To me, time was a most precious commodity and it would be criminal to waste it. Further, I discovered that time was extendable— it could be expanded to accommodate any urgent undertaking.

I believe there are three requisites for a successful life. First, the right genes—if fate deals you bad ones, you won't get to first base. Second, mental and physical self-discipline. Mental, to regulate and direct your activities, and physical to maintain health and to protect your body from excesses of food, liquor or drugs. Third, good luck. Lucky breaks are a feature of the lives of great achievers.

DR MEL POLON

Australian paediatrician

When my patients offer me their hands and thank me I feel a deep sense of satisfaction, and this, together with all that I do for those close to me, is the meaning of my life. For myself, however, the sense of meaning comes from something much deeper—it comes when I feel non-judging, unconditional love.

Watching babies can teach us a lot about being in the present and about non-judging, unconditional love. Babies bring their whole being into what they are doing at any particular moment. They do not hold onto their fears and judge, so their love is unconditional. When they feel bad or scared, they cry with all their might and then get over it and come back into the present moment again. Once while watching my son as a baby, I had a thought that he was connected to everybody in the whole world and anybody would be able to comfort him if he was distressed.

Watching babies also makes me realise how important it is to cry. When fear and sadness come to us, the only way forward is to open our hearts and accept those feelings.

PETER HARAN

Author and journalist Sunday Mail, Adelaide

I thought I had made a life-changing discovery when I realised if I changed my attitude I could change my life. Years later I found in one of those two dollar self-help books the quote by William James, 'The greatest discovery of my generation is that a human being can alter his life by altering his attitude.'

The reason I felt it was so important was because I am a Vietnam veteran—I endured and survived a war. The scar tissue I carried for years afterwards triggered bitterness and rage, which were hard to deal with. I was helped over the crisis by other veterans, but still I had to change myself; I had to change my attitude towards life and all of its sharp corners.

It is an ongoing battle to flick the on/off switch when faced with everyday conflict. However, changing attitudes—accepting the bad as well as the good, and turning tough times around—makes me a better person. It also buttresses self-belief and self-confidence, and that's something I can rub off onto others.

CLIVE WILLIAMS

Director of Terrorism Studies, Strategic and Defence Studies Centre, Canberra

I have worked on terrorism issues for nearly twenty-five years, so I have focused much of my life on desperate people and politically motivated violence. This has made me appreciate, all the more, how fortunate Australians are to live in the lucky country.

As an educator, I try to publicise and make people aware of the grievances that have led to terrorism around the world, as a way of trying to get societies to engage in constructive dialogue and longer term resolution of societal grievances, rather than simply going down the 'crush' dissent route.

I also feel strongly about the welfare of animals and contribute to an overseas animal charity; sometime in the future I would like to become more actively involved in promoting animal welfare in Asia. Meanwhile, the best advice I can give on coping with terrorism is, 'Presence of mind is good—but absence of body is better!'

HELEN REDDY

Singer and songwriter

What I always told my children is that anything of a material nature—house, car, job etc.—can be lost or taken away from you. But your experience can never be taken away from you. It is your only true wealth and will enable you to live a life rich in experience.

CHARLES BIRCH

Emeritus Professor, University of Sydney

We can change the world. But we have to have ideas that fill us with enthusiasm. We need purpose and passion together with the know-how. We don't have to wait for the whole world to change.

I have never forgotten what Margaret Mead said: 'Never doubt what a small group of thoughtful and committed citizens can do to change the world. Indeed, it is the only thing that ever has.'

It may seem difficult to hope when all seems to be against hope. Remember South Africa under apartheid? What helped many in that situation was the oft-repeated affirmation, 'Hope is believing in spite of evidence and watching the evidence change.'

DR PENNY OLSEN

*Visiting Fellow, School of Botany and Zoology,
Australian National University, Canberra*

I grew up with the feminist movement, believing in its principles but not in myself. Escape from a mired marriage unleashed a surprising strength, confidence and even wisdom. From the fullness of freedom, I gained an appreciation of the small things—a shared meal, the crisp, clean Canberra air, an azure fairy-wren against a terracotta pot, the feather dropped in my garden by a visiting sparrowhawk, a peregrine slicing the intense blue sky, a boobook singing in my street. Love and enjoyment of work for wildlife, of family, friends and foremost, my children. That was my epiphany and these are the things that sustain me.

MARA MOUSTAFINE

Author and National Director of Amnesty International Australia

I am fortunate to now work for Amnesty International, a global movement committed to exposing human rights abuses against individuals wherever they occur, with the conviction that action by ordinary people can make a difference.

In these times of global turmoil and uncertainty, it is particularly important that we all rise above our fears, celebrate our diversity and our common humanity and have the courage to strive for a better world.

DR JOHAN GALTUNG, PhD

*Professor of Peace Studies and Director of TRANSCEND,
a peace and development network*

Peace should generally not be left to generals, they are only concerned with winning and imposing something. And it is not very diplomatic to leave peace to diplomats; they also have something else on top of their agendas—the national interests. Peace has to do with world interests, human interests and nature's interest.

Peace, of course, includes the absence of direct violence; or ceasefire. That is also known as the peace of the cemetery.

Peace also includes the absence of structural violence and economic and political exploitation. And the absence of cultural violence—all the aspects of our culture that glorify direct and structural violence. But all this negative peace could also mean isolation.

Enters positive peace. Peace is the direct result of mutual harmony and cooperation; the peace structures of equity, equal exchange; and the peace culture of equality, equal dignity, equal rights. This applies to relations between civilisations and regions, nations and states, classes and genders and generations inside a society—between parents and children, between spouses, inside each human being.

Peace is the way.

LAURIE LEVY

Campaign Director, Coalition Against Duck Shooting, Australia

I believe it is important for us all to challenge injustices; to speak out for other people and other species who do not have the ability to defend themselves. Harnessing public opinion, reaching the hearts of the people and creating a groundswell of public concern through peaceful means is imperative in bringing about cultural change in our society.

The media is the most powerful weapon in fighting injustices. Over the last twenty years, media images and words portraying the brutality inflicted on defenceless native waterbirds by shooters in Australia have led to the activity being banned in two states and on the verge of being banned in another. Public opinion has again brought about a major cultural shift in our community. An activity that was considered acceptable a decade or so ago is no longer acceptable today.

A few hundred years ago Shakespeare observed that the pen was mightier than the sword. However, in today's world, the camera and its images are a far more powerful weapon than the gun.

RABBI RAYMOND APPLE, AM, RFD

Senior Rabbi of the Great Synagogue, Sydney

'Life' in Hebrew is *chayyim*—a plural word. In one sense this means that everybody sees, lives and understands life differently. No one's life is a carbon copy of anyone else's—nor should it be: as I can only be me, so you can only be you. Life is plural, but each of us is singular.

In another sense, the plural concept tells me that life is three tenses: past, present and future. The past is history—it fascinates me but I cannot change or rewrite it. The present is opportunity—as long as today lasts, I dare not waste it. The future is destiny—it intrigues me. I would love to know what life will bring. But I can help to shape and influence it by using today wisely and creatively.

JOHN BERRYMAN

Chief Executive, Royal Institute for Deaf and Blind Children, Australia

In earlier times—and still to this day in many parts of the world—to have a disability has meant having a far different life. The person with intellectual impairment would become the village idiot, Brueghel's painting depicts the plight of 'the blind leading the blind', and Dr Johnson called deafness 'one of the most desperate calamities'.

It does not have to be so. Accepting individual differences is a part of being civilised. Having inclusive schools and workplaces benefits us all. Designing built environments using sensitivity and imagination helps everybody, from wheelchair users to parents pushing strollers. Good lighting and acoustics make life easier. We make a huge positive difference to the lives of people with disabilities when we respond to their special needs in appropriate ways.

Creating and running good educational programs that will minimise the negative impact of disability is meaningful. So too is changing lives for the better by capitalising on the benefits of newborn screening, early and accurate diagnosis, and special technology.

Being part of the team that has helped the bright, but deaf, young man get to university instead of into an unskilled job is rewarding. So is watching a young blind woman become a computer programmer. These things give purpose.

PROFESSOR GRAHAME WEBB

*Conservationist and wildlife management consultant,
Northern Territory, Australia*

That the worst environmental threat is poverty is obvious but chilling. Obvious, because if we slipped towards poverty ourselves at some stage we would start killing critically endangered animals to feed our children.

Chilling, because the time scale required to solve the problems of global poverty are an order of magnitude greater than those needed to solve today's wildlife conservation problems. Those living in poverty are often cast as poachers and brigands—the enemies of conservation. But are they anything other than victims of some cruel socio-economic game?

To engage local people in conservation action, they must benefit from their efforts rather than be penalised for trying to survive. Underlying our efforts should be a simple philosophy: tolerance, respect and understanding of all peoples, cultures and traditions.

TAI PENG WANG

Writer and poet, Vancouver, Canada

I am fortunate that I am gifted with the creative talents to create spiritual wealth. This is the gift that gives meaning to my life and my happiness and fulfilment so far. This is the path I am on no matter how quiet, lonely or as dark inside as a prison cell that I sometimes feel.

This is the way to truth and meaning which I have been pursuing all my life. The late Australian poet A.D. Hope was a good friend of mine and I agree with the words from his poem 'The Tiger': 'And should he spare you in his wrath, the world and all the worlds are yours. I too am of that royal race who do what we are born to do.'

BO KJELLEN

*Former ambassador and senior adviser to the
Ministry for the Environment, Sweden*

Most of my professional life has been spent on international cooperation. I have a strong personal attachment to the idea of multilateral institutions. They are as yet relatively weak, as we can see from the state of the world, but they carry the hope of a better future. And therefore I am glad to have been given the opportunity to play an active, and sometimes leading, role in negotiations for the climate and desertification conventions, trying to improve conditions for people living far away from the meeting rooms, showing concern for the unseen. At the same time, I have one great regret: that I did not spend more time with my children when they were small.

When you get old, it is natural to look back and try to sum up your life in this way. But life carries on, and I am happy that my work on sustainable development has forced me to think deep into the future, far beyond my own short life span. Our generation is the first one whose actions and non-actions will be decisive for the wellbeing of all future generations at the global level. It is the kind of responsibility that we have to accept fully. It is the kind of responsibility that adds to the meaning of our existence, a deep sense of solidarity with the yet unborn.

JIM CONRAD

Naturalist, writer and hermit, Mississippi

Being an environmentalist in a world where the effects of blind consumerism are destroying nature, being a vegetarian in a hamburger-obsessed society, and being non-violent in a country that often seems to spoil for a fight, a few years ago I was feeling a bit overwhelmed. Then one day I heard a famous philosopher claim that the invention of the Internet might someday be judged to be as historically important as the invention of the book. This caused me to set about to master the Internet, to see what I could do to further my causes.

I pulled a tiny trailer into the forest, lived very simply, and learned Internet basics. Eight years later, using outdated computers at the end of miles of corroded Mississippi copper wire, and a very slow modem, I have created a website promoting only very small-scale, locally produced, low impact ecotourism worldwide.

PETER MALCOLM

Antarctic adventurer, speaker, workshop and Project Director of INSPIRE!, Melbourne

We are blasted from all sides with images, words, advertising, spin, emails, cyberspace, deadlines, mortgages and life in a materialistic world, which is often defined by everything outside ourselves. When I look out there I feel a rising madness, a disconnectedness with who I really am. If we get sucked into the vortex of this culture without grounding ourselves, it's a disjointed ride of heartlessness.

The more blasting I get from 'out there' the more I need to go inside, to feel my heart and what it is telling me. Slowly, I am learning to tell the difference between what my mind wants and what my heart is telling me. I know when I look into the eyes of my sparkling three-year-old twins, that they are close to spirit. I feel absolute joy in my heart and that is where I need to be to balance the craziness outside. Turn down the madness and go inside. For therein lies the glory of God in all of us, waiting patiently to communicate with us whenever we can be still enough to listen.

JAMES NICHOLS

Press Officer, Médecins sans Frontières (Doctors Without Borders), Australia

I have always believed in helping others and being an honest person. I think that as long as you are honest to yourself and the people you come into contact with, then that is all that really matters. Having visited some countries for the humanitarian organisations I have been involved with over the past seven years, such as Rwanda, Pakistan, Angola, Thailand, Laos and Burma, I have found that the spirit of cooperation and getting on in difficult circumstances is the easiest mantra to follow. I don't follow profit, results and the belief that you must make other people happy. I have found my limits, stretched them when possible and recognised when I could not go any further.

I am looking forward to making my life even more worthwhile and meaningful in years to come by getting married, having children and surfing as many waves as possible.

DR KISHO KUROKAWA

Japanese architect

A fundamental principle of my life is the philosophy of symbiosis. This is a new concept which is contrary to the commonly followed principle of dualism.

The idea of symbiosis is to create symbiotic relations between various matters even if they are antagonistic, competitive or contradictory to each other in religion, culture or economy.

I consider the twenty-first century as an era of transition from the age of the principle of hegemony towards the age of symbiosis.

As an architect I dedicate all my projects to a theme of symbiosis between man and nature, between different cultures, man and various species, science and art, tradition and high technology.

PROFESSOR TONY THOMAS

Theoretical Physicist, Adelaide University

From sometime in high school I simply knew that my life would be devoted to the pursuit of knowledge, to the discovery of ideas, concepts and laws that were previously unknown. At university I was fascinated by biochemistry, mathematics and physics. I was drawn to physics and its drive to understand the laws that govern the one world we have been given.

I have never regretted this decision. There have been a small number of times in my life where I alone, of four billion inhabitants of this much abused planet, have understood how one small part of our universe works. There is no feeling like it.

Along the way, I have built in Adelaide a research centre in subatomic physics that is known worldwide. Almost a thousand scientists have visited Adelaide for workshops and scientific collaboration. The students, research fellows and visitors constitute a truly international community, without barriers of language, race or religion.

Perhaps the greatest discovery I have made is the wonderful sense of community that comes from being part of this network. Those links represent not just professional meetings of minds but in most cases genuine friendships that continue to survive years of separation and thousands of kilometres, not to mention differences in culture and background. To be part of such a community is a real privilege.

REVEREND MIKE SEMMLER

President of the Lutheran Church of Australia

As a Christian, I consider that blessings abound and that each new day provides opportunity to set about pronouncing what God keeps announcing, and distributing what he keeps contributing.

DR HOSEN KIAT

Preventative cardiologist and author, Sydney

I overheard a conversation when a guy said to his girlfriend, 'I will do it. When I get the right opportunity.' They were discussing his idea of attending a course to advance his professional expertise as a motor mechanic.

This young man was waiting for the right opportunity. He was relying on fate. Yet fate and free-will are merely attitudes. In fate we await opportunity and in free-will, we create opportunity. Luck, it has been said, is when preparedness meets opportunity. When we undertake to create our own opportunity luck comes readily. It has no choice; it will roll at your feet in blissful abundance.

MARIA McCARTHY

Architectural lighting designer, Melbourne

The direction of my life changed dramatically one night whilst out jogging. A motor vehicle smashed my body to pieces and my emotional, mental and spiritual worlds were in smithereens as well. Curiously, that evening I was handed many gifts.

I discovered I was the fortunate recipient of unconditional love. I began to understand the importance of a loving and supportive partner, family and friends. I suffered excruciating pain, terror, sadness, vulnerability, despair and loneliness. Yet the journey from hospital to the rehabilitation unit to home was also strewn with episodes of happiness and honesty as I came to better understand my interpersonal relationships and myself. I began to cherish the feeling of sheer bliss in my regained movement and eyesight. Immobility and double vision can be very scary.

Chance changed my priorities. My life purpose, once taken for granted, changed with the impact of steel on my body. Some of these changes happened quickly, others have come more gradually, as I've reassessed my purpose in life. I have had to make adjustments that have proved to be varied—complex, taxing, yet rewarding as well. I was pushed out of my comfort zone. It is now harder for me to be complacent about life. I am a more grateful person.

DR RAYMOND GARRIES

Psychologist, Educator and Emeritus Professor,
University of Pittsburgh, Pennsylvania

Why do people see some things but not others, hear some things but not others, experience some things but not others? Perhaps it is the way for our individuality to unfold and manifest our true self.

For some, these experiences may lead to lasting happiness; for others, it may lead to disorientation, nervousness, stress, or lack of focus. Still others, and perhaps the majority of people, will fall somewhere in the middle of the extremes, neither happy nor disoriented but still separated from our true self. Nonetheless, our remarkable resilient nature keeps us moving right on through life. The struggle involved connecting with the true purpose of life—to find happiness.

Most of us look to the world of things external to ourselves—for example, possessions, work, recognition, education, physical appearance, relationships, personal or family history—for purpose. Specifically, we have an external focus. So we become confused in pursuit of real but lasting happiness. The confusion, however, is what keeps us motivated, but the continual lack of connecting with our 'true' life purpose keeps us weary about life. I have discovered that when I keep my consciousness focused on my internal self and develop a positive loving relationship with my internal self, my attitude is positive about life. On the other hand, when I keep an external focus, my attitude is wearier about life.

Moreover, with an internal focus, I tend to make fewer judgments of other people, things and especially myself. Making judgments is a major destroyer of one's peace, happiness or joy. Judgments may be rather obvious and conscious, or quite subtle and unconscious. An internal focus puts me in touch with my internal self and I have more enduring happiness. I see better, feel better, love better, and I am all around more balanced and harmonised with my internal self. In short, I spring out of bed excited to be a part of my day as it unfolds.

COLONEL JOHN BLASHFORD SNELL

Chairman, Scientific Exploration Society, and youth worker

The best advice I can give anyone seeking a meaningful life is that when young you may not have much money but you've probably got your health, vigour, energy and relatively few responsibilities. So take the opportunity when you leave school to see the world, go on an expedition, meet new people, listen to their views—even if you don't agree with them. At the same time, try to do something, however small, to make the world a better place.

Today people are healthier and live longer, and older folk have experience and wisdom that can be of real benefit in helping developing nations, the environment, wildlife conservation or in fighting disease. Even if you are not naturally outward bound, you can assist people all over the world and have fun doing it. So join a worthwhile project or start one. Youth is a state of mind.

RUSS AND BLYTH CARPENTER

Authors of The Blessings Of Bhutan, Oregon

This is a 'we' statement because after forty years of marriage, we have helped each other shape a commonly held perspective. With each passing year, we feel less comfortable about grand generalisations on the state of the world. Maybe others are able to think on that scale, but every time we give it a try we feel foolish.

For us, the internal struggle is enough. Are we learning to let go of attachments? Do we find value in the moment? How can we learn to live compassionately, setting aside prejudice and honouring all human beings?

ANTHONY PAYNE

British composer

As a happy philistine aged ten, I cared for little apart from following Arsenal Football Club and pretending I was Compton or Bradman with a bat and ball in my back garden. Then one day I heard something on the radio that utterly changed my life. There was little serious music in my household, no talk of composers or pieces, yet quite suddenly a few seconds of music, which of course I neither knew nor really 'understood', made me feel I was floating above the clouds.

Was it a mystical experience—certainly a seed had been planted, but by whom? I became an obsessive listener to classical music, and eventually discovered the passage which had transformed me was the opening of Brahms' First Symphony. I began to realise that I'd discovered my pathway: to live physically and spiritually in the world of music. This soon became a determination to compose and, who knows, perhaps even affect others the way I'd been affected.

I feel blessed to have been mysteriously and inexplicably claimed by music, and finding that it made sense of the world's chaos. I also wanted to spread a love and understanding of it. Music revealed the vastness of the cosmos, and made me realise humankind's insignificance in the grand scheme of things—a useful antidote to hubris.

In truth, music has given me a reason for living; but no less important has been my long-standing marriage to soprano Jane Manning, who has remained sweetheart, friend and musical colleague. In sum, music and love of another human being have led to a life of spiritual adventure and, I firmly believe, fulfilment.

GARRY WEARE

*Author, adventurer, long-term resident of Kashmir
and a director of the Australian Himalayan Foundation*

Having lived for many years in the Himalaya, people assume that I must be a New Age guru with an answer for everything. How wrong can they be!

The longer I lived in Kashmir, the more I trekked over high passes, the longer I gazed at high mountains, the more I realised that I didn't have a clue about the purpose of my life, the afterlife, or anyone else's for that matter.

If we can discover whether life has a purpose—and I am not convinced there is one—then it is to keep an open mind; listen to those with true vision and above all try to ask the right questions that may get you a little nearer to anything resembling the truth.

ABLE SEAMAN ROBERT 'BOB' COLLINS

*ASDIC operator, survivor of two ship sinkings during World War II—
HMAS Perth and Rakuyo Maru—and POW on the
Thai-Burma railway, Queensland*

'The Aussies never gave up, and never let you down.' My brother once sent me a cutting from the *Sydney Morning Herald* about a survey done at the Australian National University which said that during the war, 'No Australian died alone'. We looked after each other. I washed and bathed blokes, and held their hands when they were dying. I washed their bandages and fixed up their legs for them. And they did the same for me. They were wonderful men. One day a bloke came over to me and said, 'Do you mind if I have your rice?' Of course I gave it to him. That was typical of the POWs. They were polite and generous even under the most terrible circumstances.

CHRIS 'DORJE' WALKER

Surfer and author, Bondi Beach, Australia

There is an expression that tourists don't know where they have been and travellers don't know where they are going. For me in India many years ago, I felt like I was slowly making the transition between being a tourist and a traveller. Where was I going? I didn't know. All I had was my intention and a sense of purpose. I was on a mission to find my teacher and I was prepared to go anywhere and do anything to find him or her.

My purpose was to learn so that I may share that wisdom with others, and perhaps if I learnt well enough and through dedication and tireless effort I may make such an impact that they may go on to teach others—a somewhat idealistic dream but it was all that I wanted to do. My soul purpose, you might say.

So I had interviews with abbots of monasteries and lamas of various traditions. I was looking for the most qualified teacher I could find and at the same time I knew nothing of what I was looking for. I had no way to tell a good teacher from an inadequate teacher. No way to know a true teacher from a phoney. Perhaps if they had light shining from their eyes or could tell me who I was in my former life and what I was looking for…but none of that was likely to happen.

Here I was, the blind leading myself along a road at night, trying to find my way. It brings to mind Shantideva, a great India yogi and scholar who I was to learn about later in my studies. He had a marvellous saying, along the lines of: 'It is like you are walking through the hills in the middle of the night, lost trying to find your way. And then a flash of lightning lights up the night sky and it all becomes clear just for a few moments so that you can get your bearings once again and continue upon your way.'

I think in moments when I have been looking for an answer or for a reason to go on, I am lucky because I now know that lightning will come, sooner or later, if I just stay put and wait.

NAOMI WOLF

American author and feminist

The best advice I could give is one that my teacher of Buddhist ethics, Sharon Salzberg, passed on to me: 'Assume that everyone you meet is fighting a mighty battle.'

PROFESSOR MARGARET REYNOLDS

National President, United Nations of Australia

My work over more than forty years has constantly reminded me that society is divided by those people who are denied equality, and those who arrogantly demand more than their fair share. Ideally, a well-organised society will protect its vulnerable members and share the benefits in the interests of all. However, increasingly there is withdrawal of government from social services and open encouragement of a culture of selfishness.

This level of greed is exacerbated globally while Westerners demand their right to maintain a lifestyle of plenty while millions live in poverty. Within developing nations the poor suffer while corruption abounds.

We know this future is both unsustainable and amoral, yet how do we institute change that places priority on human worth?

Those of us who enjoy such a wealth of opportunity and resources have an obligation to advocate reform of social values which could enable all peoples access to a decent standard of living. Ultimately, the kind of future we share depends on our commitment to social justice.

BROTHER HOWARD

Little Brothers of Francis, Franciscan Hermitage, Tabulam, Australia

Thoreau, in his book *On Walden Pond*, wrote that he had wanted to live life deliberately. To live deliberately is to make conscious choices of how to live one's life. We all make choices that make a difference in our own lives and in the lives of others, from how we treat other people and how we use our money to how we make time in our lives for what is really important.

This may mean some things have to go! I have consciously chosen to be a disciple of Christ, to be a Franciscan Brother, to live simply; to do some manual work every day; to be open to the opportunities God places in my way; and to enjoy it all.